HYDROFRACKING
THE PROCESS THAT HAS CHANGED AMERICA'S ENERGY NEEDS

BY ANN O. SQUIRE

W9-AOS-870

CHILDREN'S PRESS®
An Imprint of Scholastic Inc.
New York Toronto London Auckland Sydney
Mexico City New Delhi Hong Kong
Danbury, Connecticut

BRINGING HISTORY to LIFE

Content Consultant
James Marten, PhD
Professor and Chair, History Department
Marquette University
Milwaukee, Wisconsin

Library of Congress Cataloging-in-Publication Data

Squire, Ann.
  Hydrofracking / by Ann O. Squire.
     pages cm.—(Cornerstones of freedom)
  Audience: 9–12.
  Audience: Grade 4 to 6
  Includes bibliographical references and index.
  ISBN 978-0-531-23604-8 (lib. bdg.) — ISBN 978-0-531-21962-1 (pbk.)
  1. Gas well drilling—Juvenile literature. 2. Shale gas—Juvenile literature.
3. Hydraulic fracturing—Juvenile literature. I. Title.
  TN880.2.S687 2013
  622'.3385—dc23   2012034322

All rights reserved. Published in 2013 by Children's Press, an imprint of
Scholastic Inc.
Printed in the United States of America 113

SCHOLASTIC, CHILDREN'S PRESS, CORNERSTONES OF FREEDOM™,
and associated logos are trademarks and/or registered trademarks of
Scholastic Inc.

1 2 3 4 5 6 7 8 9 10 R 22 21 20 19 18 17 16 15 14 13

Photographs © 2013: Alamy Images: 6, 14, 57 top (Everett Collection
Inc.), 5 bottom, 44, 57 bottom (Lebrecht Music and Arts Photo Library);
AP Images: 2, 3, 4 bottom, 4 top, 7, 8, 10, 11, 12, 17, 18, 20, 21, 22, 23, 24,
28, 30, 32, 33, 34, 36, 37, 38, 45, 48, 51 (North Wind Picture Archives), 39
(Osamu Honda), 55 (Paul Beaty); Courtesy of John Carter Brown Library at
Brown University: 5 top, 47; Media Bakery/Kristy-Anne Glubish: cover; The
Colonial Williamsburg Foundation: back cover; The Granger Collection:
40 (John Smibert), 46 (Noel Le Mire after Louis Lepaon), 50, 56 (Susan
Sedgwick), 13, 26; The Image Works: 29 (AAAC/Topham), 42 (Mary Evans
Picture Library), 54 (Topham).

Maps by XNR Productions, Inc.

Did you know that studying history can be fun?

BRING HISTORY TO LIFE by becoming a history investigator. Examine the evidence (primary and secondary source materials); cross-examine the people and witnesses. Take a look at what was happening at the time—but be careful! What happened years ago might suddenly become incredibly interesting and change the way you think!

Contents

4

SETTING THE SCENE
Fossil Fuels

TVs, computers, cell phones, and other electronic devices all require energy to work.

Almost everything we do requires energy. When we ride the bus to school, warm up pizza in the microwave, switch on the lights, turn up the heat, or watch TV, we are using energy. Where does this energy come from?

Most of the energy used in the United States comes from the burning of **fossil fuels**, such as coal, oil, and natural gas. The fossil fuels we use today were created from the remains of ancient plants and animals. As these **organic** materials decomposed, they were gradually covered up by layers of sand and silt. Over millions of years, the layers built up, and the dead plants and animals were buried deep underground. Intense pressure and heat transformed the sandy layers into rock and changed the organic materials into oil, coal, or natural gas.

Because fossil fuels take so long to form, they are considered nonrenewable resources. Once we have used them up, they will be gone forever. Currently, about 82 percent of the nation's energy comes from fossil fuels. Because people depend so heavily on these fuels, we are always looking for new sources and easier ways to obtain them.

Americans rely on massive coal mining operations for much of their fuel.

USED EACH YEAR IN THE UNITED STATES

CHAPTER 1

OUR GROWING ENERGY NEEDS

The U.S. population grows larger every year.

THE NUMBER OF PEOPLE WHO call the United States home is growing rapidly. In the year 2000, the country was estimated to have a population of more than 281 million people. By 2010, that number had grown to more than 308 million. If current trends continue, the U.S. population will top 438 million people by 2050.

As the population grows, the country's energy needs increase. There are more buildings to heat, more machines that require electricity to run, and more vehicles on the road. Will there be enough energy to go around?

Middle Eastern nations such as Iraq are home to some of the world's largest oil supplies.

Oil and gas wells in Alaska and the lower 48 states produce some of the fuel that we need, but it is not enough. In 2011, almost half the nation's fuel was imported from foreign nations such as Iraq and Saudi Arabia. Political unrest in these countries can cause the price of oil and gas to rise sharply. If we cannot meet our own energy needs, we must pay that price, no matter how high it is.

For several decades, U.S. leaders have wanted to reduce the country's dependence on imported fuel. Achieving that goal now seems possible. A technique

A FIRSTHAND LOOK AT
PRESIDENT OBAMA'S 2012 STATE OF THE UNION ADDRESS

President Barack Obama believes that the United States should work toward energy independence. In his 2012 State of the Union address, he discussed both hydrofracking and renewable energy sources. See page 60 for a link to watch a video of the speech online.

called hydraulic fracturing, or hydrofracking, may allow us to collect all the natural gas we need for years to come. Is this new technology the answer? Or is it too good to be true?

During his 2012 State of the Union speech, President Obama stressed the importance of developing new energy sources.

Oil or Gas?

Oil is the largest single source of energy in the United States. In 2010, 37 percent of the country's energy came from oil. Much of it was imported from other countries. Natural gas provided 25 percent of our energy, and coal provided 21 percent. The remaining 17 percent came from nuclear power and renewable energy sources, such as wind, solar, and geothermal power.

There are several good reasons to use more natural gas and less coal and oil. When burned, natural gas

Vehicle emissions are a major source of air pollution in the United States.

Many stove tops use natural gas as a fuel for their flames.

releases less carbon dioxide than either coal or oil. Carbon dioxide in the atmosphere has been linked to **global warming**. By using natural gas in place of coal and oil, we can reduce the amount of carbon dioxide released into the atmosphere and slow global warming.

Coal and oil also release nitrogen oxides as well as soot and ash particles, which contribute to smog, poor air quality, and acid rain. Natural gas releases lower levels of all of these substances. Because of this, burning gas as fuel should do less harm to the air we breathe.

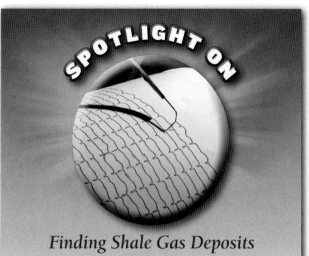

Finding Shale Gas Deposits

Geologists use **seismographs** and sophisticated computer imaging equipment to locate underground shale gas reserves. By sending sound waves into the earth and measuring how those waves are reflected back by different underground layers, the geologists can create a three-dimensional image of rock formations beneath the surface. Computer imaging helps to give a detailed view of underground gas deposits, rock thickness, natural fractures, underground water, and more.

Different underground formations and rock types also have different effects on the earth's magnetic and gravitational fields. Geologists look at small changes in these fields to get a better idea of what lies below the surface. Drilling companies use all this information to place wells where gas reserves are richest.

One of the best reasons to increase the use of natural gas is that we have large amounts of it in our own backyard. Using natural gas in place of oil would help reduce our dependence on foreign energy.

An Ocean of Gas

Beneath the deserts of the American Southwest and stretching from Texas all the way into New York State lie huge reserves of natural gas. In 2011, the United States Energy Information Administration estimated that these lands contained enough natural gas to provide the country with energy for almost 100 years. If we have so much gas here at home, why are we still importing fuel from overseas?

Much of our country's gas reserves are in the form of shale gas. Shale gas is natural gas that is stored within a claylike **sedimentary rock** called shale. Shale is filled with many small pores, and natural gas is found inside these tiny spaces. A shale deposit may contain huge quantities of natural gas, but it cannot easily flow out because it is trapped within the tiny shale pores. Conventional drilling techniques do not work well in these situations. They produce only a small amount of natural gas.

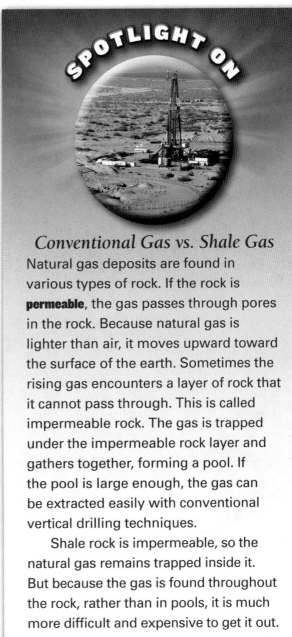

SPOTLIGHT ON

Conventional Gas vs. Shale Gas

Natural gas deposits are found in various types of rock. If the rock is **permeable**, the gas passes through pores in the rock. Because natural gas is lighter than air, it moves upward toward the surface of the earth. Sometimes the rising gas encounters a layer of rock that it cannot pass through. This is called impermeable rock. The gas is trapped under the impermeable rock layer and gathers together, forming a pool. If the pool is large enough, the gas can be extracted easily with conventional vertical drilling techniques.

Shale rock is impermeable, so the natural gas remains trapped inside it. But because the gas is found throughout the rock, rather than in pools, it is much more difficult and expensive to get it out.

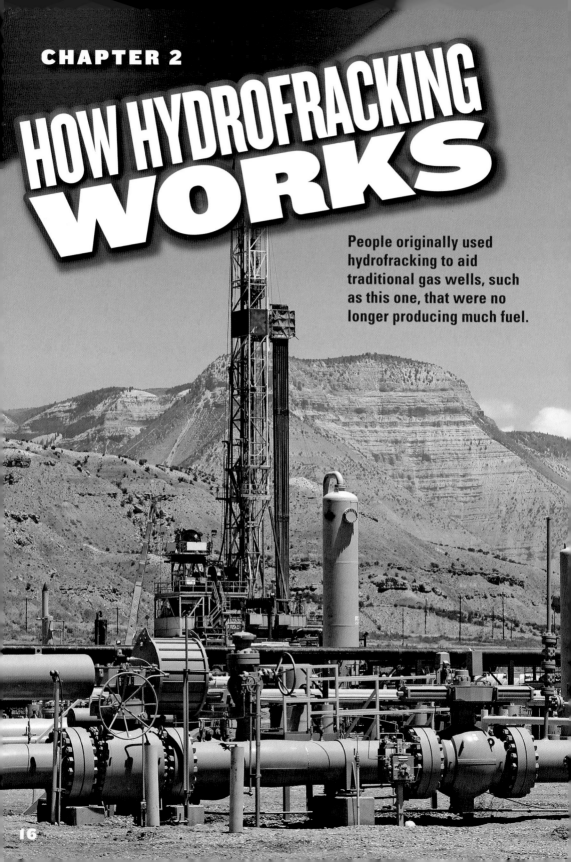

CHAPTER 2

HOW HYDROFRACKING WORKS

People originally used hydrofracking to aid traditional gas wells, such as this one, that were no longer producing much fuel.

HYDROFRACKING HAS BEEN used since the 1860s to reactivate oil and gas wells that seemed to be running dry. By pumping liquids into a well at high pressure, drillers discovered that they could create cracks in the underground rock and release trapped oil and gas. At first, hydrofracking was only used to increase the production of existing oil and gas wells. But eventually, people realized that hydrofracking might be a good way to access natural gas trapped inside shale deposits.

The Barnett Shale remains an important source of natural gas in the United States.

In the 1980s, Mitchell Energy, a drilling company founded by an engineer named George Mitchell, began to experiment with hydrofracking to stimulate gas production in the Barnett Shale. This was a large shale deposit in Texas known to have huge gas reserves. Because all the gas was trapped inside the shale deposits, no wells had been very successful. Mitchell Energy used hydrofracking to unlock the Barnett Shale's rich gas deposits. Many other companies followed suit.

Hydrofracking was soon being used to drill for natural gas in Louisiana, Arkansas, Pennsylvania, and several other states. By 2010, there were close to 500,000 natural gas wells across the United States.

Anatomy of a Gas Well

Shale gas deposits are usually found deep below the earth's surface. Sometimes they are as much as a mile underground. The first step in obtaining the shale gas is to drill a vertical well. After clearing a large area, workers lay a waterproof liner to protect the ground from spills and wastewater

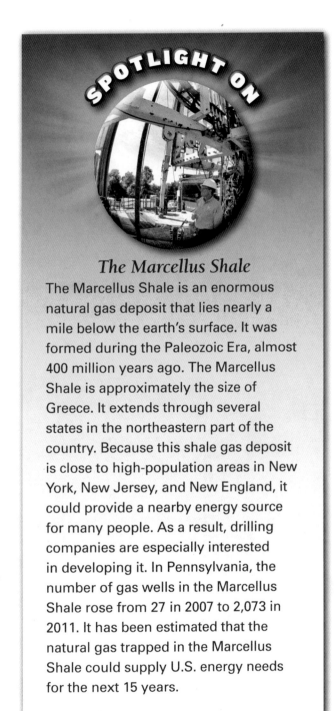

SPOTLIGHT ON

The Marcellus Shale

The Marcellus Shale is an enormous natural gas deposit that lies nearly a mile below the earth's surface. It was formed during the Paleozoic Era, almost 400 million years ago. The Marcellus Shale is approximately the size of Greece. It extends through several states in the northeastern part of the country. Because this shale gas deposit is close to high-population areas in New York, New Jersey, and New England, it could provide a nearby energy source for many people. As a result, drilling companies are especially interested in developing it. In Pennsylvania, the number of gas wells in the Marcellus Shale rose from 27 in 2007 to 2,073 in 2011. It has been estimated that the natural gas trapped in the Marcellus Shale could supply U.S. energy needs for the next 15 years.

runoff. Next, a drilling pad is constructed and a drill rig is set up. Other equipment and supplies are brought in. Finally, drilling begins. The drill passes through layers of sandstone, limestone, and other rock. It may also pass through **aquifers** that serve as sources of drinking water before reaching the shale deposit. At this point, the drill turns 90 degrees and bores through the shale rock horizontally for several thousand feet.

When drilling is complete, a steel pipe called a casing is lowered into the well and cemented into place. The casing is designed to create a barrier between the well and the surrounding earth, so that water, chemicals, and

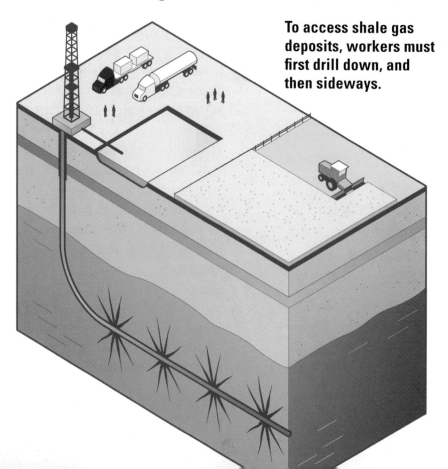

To access shale gas deposits, workers must first drill down, and then sideways.

natural gas do not leak from the well into the ground or aquifers.

Next, a device called a perforating gun is dropped into the well. When it reaches the bottom, it turns and slides along the horizontal portion of the well until it gets to the end. Triggered by workers thousands of feet above, the gun fires. Explosions blast holes in the steel casing and the cement, making large cracks in the surrounding rock. This process is repeated along the length of the well, until the casing is peppered with holes and the shale rock is cracked in thousands of spots.

YESTERDAY'S HEADLINES

In 1974, Congress passed the Safe Drinking Water Act. Its purpose was to ensure safe drinking water for all Americans. It gave the Environmental Protection Agency (EPA) the authority to set standards for potential contaminants to drinking water. Thirty years later, Vice President Dick Cheney pushed to make oil and gas drilling companies exempt from the Safe Drinking Water Act. In 2005, Congress agreed with Cheney and passed the Energy Policy Act. This amendment took away the EPA's authority to regulate the liquids and chemicals used in hydrofracking. Since 2005, the gas industry has been allowed to use whatever chemicals it wants in the hydrofracking process, even if these chemicals are harmful or used near underground drinking water supplies.

Workers use tanker trucks to transport fracking chemicals to drilling sites.

The hydrofracking process begins after the perforating gun has been removed. Workers at the drilling site use high-pressure pumps to force a mixture of water, chemicals, and sand or small ceramic beads down into the well. This mixture is called fracking fluid. It passes through the steel pipe and out into the cracks in the rock that have been created by the perforating gun. Under intense pressure from the liquid, the cracks widen. As the water flows into the cracks, the sand or beads are carried along and deposited there. These "proppants" hold the cracks open when the water is gone.

When no more water can be pumped into the hole, the pumps are switched off. Natural pressure forces some of the liquid to flow out of the cracks and back through the pipe to the surface. Usually, only about half of the liquid is recovered. The rest remains underground.

Millions of gallons of water may be used in a hydrofracking operation. This creates several challenges. The first is obtaining the large amount of water that is needed for the fracking fluid. In many cases, water is taken from rivers, streams, reservoirs, or other water sources near the site. If there is no water source nearby, the drilling company may build pipelines to bring in the water, or the water may be transported to the drilling site by tanker truck.

Huge hoses are sometimes used to connect drilling sites to water sources.

Wastewater is held in pits near the drilling site.

Another challenge involves dealing with the wastewater (also called produced water) that comes back up after drilling is complete. It is sometimes stored

A FIRSTHAND LOOK AT
A REPORT ON CHEMICALS USED IN HYDRAULIC FRACTURING

In 2011, the U.S. House of Representatives Committee on Energy and Commerce asked oil and gas companies for information on chemicals typically used in hydraulic fracturing. The report notes that the added chemicals ranged from harmless to extremely toxic. In some cases, the gas drillers could not even identify the chemicals that they had used. See page 60 for a link to read the committee's report online.

At water treatment facilities, water is cleaned before being released back into the natural environment.

in open pits at the drilling site. The water may also be taken by truck to various treatment facilities, or it may be injected deep underground into disposal wells. Because of the large volume of wastewater and the chemicals it contains, all of these methods present some hazards to people and to the environment.

As the wastewater recedes, natural gas that has been trapped in the shale rock begins to flow into the cracks, through the pipe, and up to the collection well. The proppants continue to hold the cracks open so that the gas can escape and rise up to the surface.

CHAPTER 3

PROTECTING THE ENVIRONMENT

The burning of fossil fuels releases dangerous chemicals into the air.

HYDROFRACKING HAS CAUSED a lot of controversy. People in favor of developing natural gas resources point out that gas is a clean-burning fuel. It does not contribute to air pollution, smog, or acid rain as much as other fossil fuels do. Supporters of hydrofracking also note the ample supply of gas reserves in the United States. This would mean lower energy bills for millions of Americans.

Residents of DeWitt, New York, gather to debate the pros and cons of allowing hydrofracking in their community.

Many people, however, do not believe that the benefits of natural gas outweigh the risks that come with hydrofracking. These risks include chemical pollution of drinking water sources, threats to the health of people living near gas wells, and even earthquakes.

Questionable Chemicals

Fracking fluid contains water and either sand or ceramic beads. It also contains a variety of chemicals, including acids to dissolve minerals and gels to thicken the fluid. Drilling companies say that the chemicals make up a very small percentage of the total fluid. Water and sand usually account for more than 98 percent of the total, with added chemicals making up the rest. At first, this sounds like an insignificant amount. But a typical hydrofracking job may use 4 million gallons (15.1 million liters) of liquid. That amount of fracking fluid could contain as much as 80,000 gallons (302,833 L) of added chemicals!

Some of the chemicals used in hydrofracking have been shown to cause cancer. Others must be disposed of as hazardous wastes. Some of the chemicals remain a mystery, because natural gas companies are not required to tell anyone exactly what chemicals they are using.

Workers use pumps to load wastewater into trucks that carry it away from drilling sites.

Water and Air Pollution

Companies that drill for shale gas have assured government agencies and the public that hydrofracking does not harm the environment. They point to safety measures ensuring that chemicals are contained within the gas wells and disposed of properly. But there are a number of stages where accidents or carelessness could result in chemical contamination.

Chemical Spills

There is the potential for chemical contamination if mistakes are made when the liner is placed under the drilling pad. Spills while mixing the fracking fluid and

Devon Energy Corporation, run by Larry Nichols (below), and other energy companies claim that hydrofracking does not harm the environment.

Fracking fluids can sometimes spill out into natural areas.

spills while transferring the fluid to storage containers are both times when chemicals could overflow the drilling pad and soak into the ground. This has been a problem at several drilling sites in Pennsylvania, where chemicals seeped into a creek and killed a large number of fish.

Leaky Well Casings

After a well is drilled, the hole is lined with steel casings that are cemented into place. If there is a problem with the casings or any cracks in the cement, fracking fluid could leak out into the surrounding earth. A casing failure would be especially dangerous where the vertical

Scientists test water sources to make sure they do not contain harmful substances.

portion of the well passes through underground aquifers that supply drinking water. Well casing failures have already been reported at several drilling sites in Pennsylvania. These problems led to the pollution of 10 drinking water wells located near the gas wells.

Cracked well casings can also be responsible for methane leaks. Methane is the main component of natural gas. While it is not poisonous, it is highly **flammable**. High amounts of methane gas can result in explosions and fires. Methane can also displace oxygen from the air, causing breathing problems or even death. A team of scientists at Duke University recently tested the drinking water from private wells in Pennsylvania and New York. Some of the wells were located close to natural gas drilling sites. Others were farther away. What they found was alarming. The water from wells near drilling sites contained 17 times as much methane as wells in non-drilling areas.

In *Gasland*, a documentary film on hydrofracking, people whose wells had been contaminated with methane and other chemicals were interviewed. They reported headaches and other symptoms. Several families had so much methane in their well water that they were able to light their tap water on fire as it came out of the faucet.

Air Pollution

After a fracking job has taken place, natural gas begins to flow from the well. The first gases to come out are not captured. They are

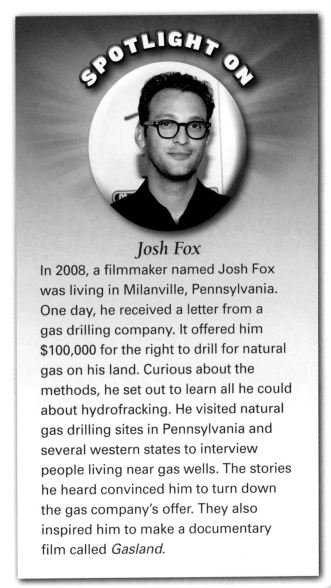

SPOTLIGHT ON

Josh Fox

In 2008, a filmmaker named Josh Fox was living in Milanville, Pennsylvania. One day, he received a letter from a gas drilling company. It offered him $100,000 for the right to drill for natural gas on his land. Curious about the methods, he set out to learn all he could about hydrofracking. He visited natural gas drilling sites in Pennsylvania and several western states to interview people living near gas wells. The stories he heard convinced him to turn down the gas company's offer. They also inspired him to make a documentary film called *Gasland*.

Gas flares are one of several ways that hydrofracking causes air pollution.

burned off in a process called flaring. Flaring releases gases and toxic compounds into the atmosphere. When these are added to fumes from **generators**, drilling rigs, and other equipment, air pollution can become a serious

A FIRSTHAND LOOK AT
FRACKNATION

There are two sides to every story. Three filmmakers—Phelim McAleer, Ann McElhinney, and Magdalena Segieda—disagree with the claims made in *Gasland*. They conducted their own interviews of people affected by hydrofracking and have raised funds to produce a film called *FrackNation*. See page 60 for a link to watch an interview with the filmmakers.

problem in areas around drilling sites. High levels of ozone, which can cause breathing problems and lung disease, have been measured at some sites. In fact, some gas drilling sites have ozone levels higher than those found in major cities.

Another source of air pollution comes from the trucks that are used to transport fresh water and equipment to drilling sites and carry wastewater away for treatment and disposal. According to Pennsylvania's Department of Environmental Protection, one hydrofracking job can require 1,000 truck trips.

Some people are also worried about the amount of methane gas that is released during and after hydrofracking. Methane is a **greenhouse gas**, which

The trucks that bring water to drilling sites cause air pollution as they burn fuel to drive.

means that it helps to trap heat in the atmosphere. This contributes to global warming. Some studies have suggested that large amounts of methane are escaping into the atmosphere as a result of shale gas drilling. So although natural gas is a cleaner-burning fuel than oil or coal, it may be polluting the air and warming our planet just as much as oil and coal are.

Fractured Shale

During hydrofracking, water, sand, and chemicals are pumped directly into cracks that have been made in shale formations. Some of this fluid flows back to the surface, but much of it remains underground. Many people believe that this fracking liquid is so far below any sources of drinking water that it cannot cause con-

Global warming is causing huge amounts of ice to melt in Antarctica, leaving less living space for animals such as polar bears.

tamination. However, others fear that the fractures in the shale created by hydro-fracking, along with natural cracks in the earth, could provide a pathway for contaminated water to seep upward to aquifers that hold drinking water.

It is not just the chemicals in fracking fluid that can cause problems. Many harmful substances are found naturally, deep below the earth's surface. Fracking fluid mixes with these substances when it is pumped into cracks in shale rock. The liquid that remains underground after a fracking job now contains these added materials. If it

SPOTLIGHT ON

Greenhouse Gases and Global Warming

Gases in the atmosphere help to keep our planet warm. Without them, the earth would be a much colder place. But too much of certain gases can make the planet too hot. This is known as global warming.

Energy from the sun causes the surface of the earth to heat up. When the earth cools down, it releases this stored energy as radiation. Some gases, such as carbon dioxide, methane, and ozone, absorb this radiation. Instead of escaping into outer space, heat is trapped in Earth's atmosphere. As the atmosphere warms, the surface of the earth gets warmer, too. Some of the effects of global warming are higher temperatures, changes in weather patterns, melting glaciers at the poles, and rising sea levels. One of the main causes of global warming today is the burning of fossil fuels.

Huge tanks are sometimes used to store produced water.

moves upward through cracks into underground water supplies, it can contaminate drinking water.

Produced Water

The liquid that comes back up after a hydrofracking job is called produced water. In addition to the chemicals added by the drilling company, this water now contains the substances picked up underground. Drilling companies deal with produced water in several ways. Sometimes it is stored in large, open pits at the drilling site. The pits are often lined with waterproof material to ensure that the produced water does not soak into the ground. But leaks can occur if the liner becomes torn or damaged. Storing the wastewater in holding ponds can also contribute to air quality problems. As the water **evaporates**, toxic chemicals are released into the air.

Another way of disposing of produced water is to transport it by truck to water treatment facilities. Unfortunately, many water treatment plants are not able to remove all the chemicals before releasing the treated water into rivers and streams.

Some drilling companies dispose of their produced water by pumping it deep underground for storage. The storage wells, called injection wells, are thousands of feet deep. Many people believe that this practice can trigger earthquakes, but that has not been definitively proven.

Large hoses help workers transfer water and chemicals from one place to another during fracking operations.

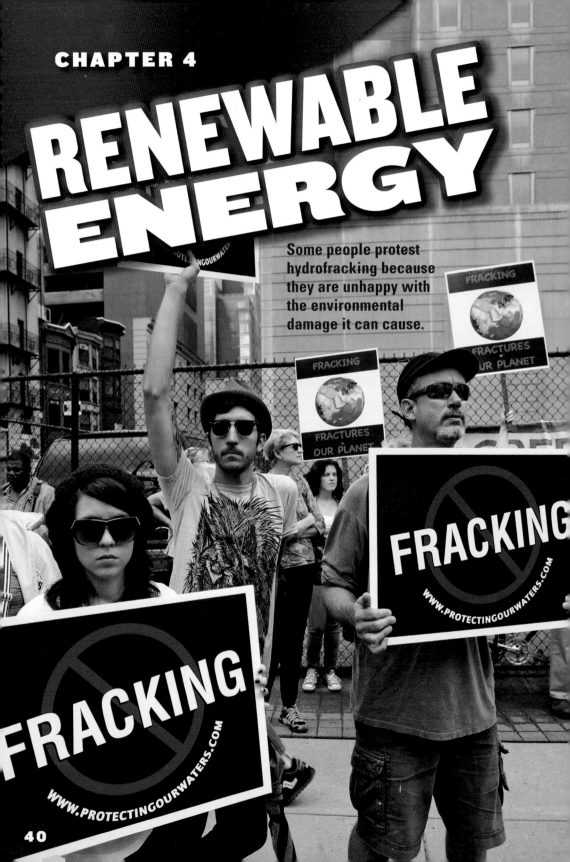

CHAPTER 4

RENEWABLE ENERGY

Some people protest hydrofracking because they are unhappy with the environmental damage it can cause.

FRACKING
FRACTURES OUR PLANET

FRACKING
FRACTURES OUR PLANET

FRACKING
WWW.PROTECTINGOURWATERS.COM

FRACKING
WWW.PROTECTINGOURWATERS.COM

DESPITE THE DANGERS TO THE environment that come with hydrofracking, shale gas is likely to become an important energy source. The federal government, along with the governments of states where hydrofracking takes place, is developing rules and regulations that will help to make this drilling technique safer.

Solar panels are one possible solution to the debate over energy sources.

But is shale gas really an answer to our country's energy needs? Although we have large gas deposits waiting to be used, those reserves will eventually run out. And while it may be cleaner than oil or coal, natural gas is still a fossil fuel. Burning natural gas or any fossil fuel contributes to global warming and all the problems that go along with it.

Renewable energy sources may be an answer. Energy that comes from the sun and wind will never run out. These are cleaner forms of energy. They usually have a smaller impact on the environment than fossil fuels. And developing its own renewable energy sources would help the United States to depend less on foreign oil and gas.

Energy from the Sun

Solar radiation is one type of renewable energy. Captured energy from the sun can be converted into heat, electricity, and other forms of energy. Photovoltaic devices, also known as solar cells, turn the sun's energy directly into electricity. Some solar cells are small, like those found in solar-powered watches or calculators. Others are grouped together into large panels that can be mounted on rooftops. In sunny areas, several large solar panels on a south-facing roof can provide enough electricity for an average single-family home.

Solar energy can also be used to heat water and produce steam, which is then used to run

A VIEW FROM ABROAD

Hydrofracking is not only an American practice. Countries around the world are considering whether to allow shale gas drilling. Poland has some of the largest shale gas deposits in Europe. It is in favor of hydrofracking and has issued permits for shale gas exploration. France and Bulgaria are more concerned about environmental impacts. They have banned the practice. The United Kingdom recently suspended hydrofracking temporarily after it was linked to a series of earthquakes. However, it began drilling again after improving safety conditions.

generators that make electricity. This process is being used at power plants across the country. In 2010, it provided most of the electricity at 13 power plants in the United States.

Solar power does have some limitations. In many areas of the country, there is not enough sunshine to produce reliable solar power. Weather and time of year are also factors affecting the amount of sunshine that reaches the earth's surface. California, Arizona, Nevada, and other areas where the sun shines most of the time are the best places to take advantage of solar energy.

Huge solar farms can capture large amounts of energy from the sun and distribute it to nearby towns.

Wind farms are one of the cleanest sources of energy available.

Energy from Wind

Wind power is another renewable energy source that is becoming more and more popular. Modern wind turbines look very different from traditional windmills,

A FIRSTHAND LOOK AT
A UN REPORT ON RENEWABLE ENERGY SOURCES

A recent report by the United Nations Environmental Programme found that switching to renewable energy sources, such as solar, wind, and geothermal energy, could help to stop global warming. The report also concluded that nearly 80 percent of the world's energy supply could be met by renewable energy sources by the middle of this century. See page 60 to read the report online.

Wind Turbine

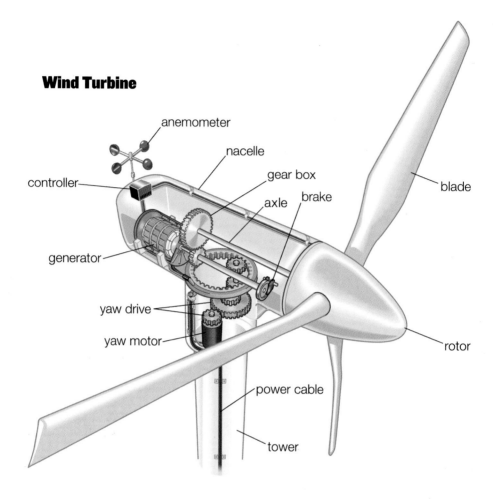

anemometer

nacelle

controller

gear box

blade

axle   brake

generator

yaw drive

yaw motor

rotor

power cable

tower

As the blades of a wind turbine spin, they generate electricity.

but they work in much the same way. The turbine's long blades catch the wind and, as they spin, they turn a long rod called an axle. The axle is connected to a generator. In this way, wind energy is converted into electricity. In 2011, enough wind energy was produced in the United States to power about 10 million homes.

Just as solar energy can only be produced when the sun shines, wind energy is only possible when the wind blows. Wind farms built on hilltops, open plains, or shorelines, or even built offshore, can capture more wind power.

Energy from the Earth

Geothermal energy comes from heat that is generated underground. The earth's mantle layer, which lies just below the crust (Earth's outer skin), is made up of very hot, melted rock called magma. Temperatures in the mantle can reach 1600 degrees Fahrenheit (871 degrees Celsius). In some places, the magma comes close to the surface of the earth. Underground rocks and water in these areas are warmed by the superheated magma.

For many years, people have harnessed this energy by digging wells and pumping heated underground steam or water to the surface. This hot water can be pumped directly into buildings to provide heat.

Hot springs are warmed naturally by the earth's interior heat.

Another way of harnessing geothermal energy is to use steam or hot water from underground to turn generators that make electricity. The United States produces a small amount of its electricity at geothermal power plants. Other countries depend more heavily on geothermal energy. A geothermal system in Reykjavík, Iceland, heats 95 percent of the city's buildings.

Geothermal energy does have some disadvantages. One is the difficulty of finding a suitable place for a geothermal power plant. A good location is one with hot underground rocks that are not too deep below the surface. A location may also run out of steam or even release hazardous gases into the environment. Despite these drawbacks, geothermal energy can be a reliable source of power in some areas.

Geothermal power plants are excellent energy sources, but are only possible in certain areas.

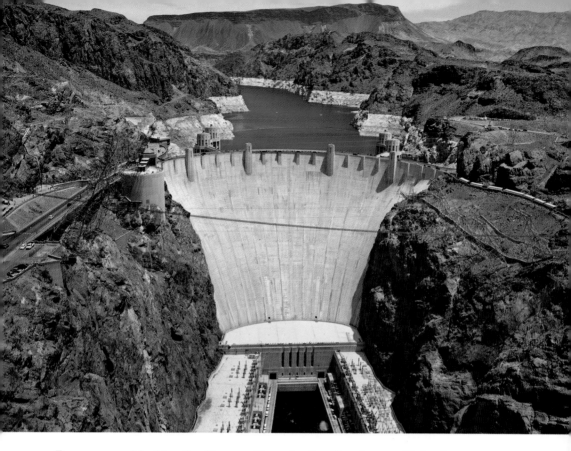

Energy provided by the Hoover Dam, in the Southwest United States, is used to power towns in several surrounding states.

Energy from Moving Water

Like wind, moving water can be harnessed to run genera-tors that produce electricity. Energy from moving water is known as hydropower. The best sources of hydropower are large, fast-flowing rivers or waterfalls. Hydroelectric dams, such as the Hoover Dam in Arizona and Nevada and the Grand Coulee Dam in Washington State, use moving water to turn turbine blades connected to generators.

While hydropower is a renewable resource, it does have environmental impacts. Dams can get in the way of fish movements. They can also affect the temperature, water chemistry, and flow rate of the rivers they are built

Some people still burn wood to heat their homes.

on. Lakes created by dams, called reservoirs, can cover up important natural areas and affect plants and wildlife.

Energy from Plants and Animals

Organic material from plants and animals is known as biomass. When people build a wood fire in the fireplace, burn leaves in the fall, or fill a gas tank with a biofuel such as ethanol, they are obtaining energy from biomass. Biomass is considered a renewable energy source because more plants and animals can always be raised.

Burning wood or other organic material is one way to get energy from biomass. Another is to convert these materials to fuels such as ethanol, biodiesel, and methane, which can then be burned.

Using biomass as an energy source can have both positive and negative impacts on the environment. Power plants that burn trash produce energy while at the same time reducing the amount of garbage that ends up in landfills. But these plants also produce air pollution and may release harmful chemicals found in the waste. Wood also releases air pollutants when burned.

Biofuels are made from plants such as corn, sugarcane, and soybeans. They are renewable and burn more cleanly than gasoline. But the land, water, fertilizers, and energy needed to grow these crops could be used to grow food crops instead.

TODAY'S PERSPECTIVE

In New York, where drilling companies hope to develop natural gas reserves contained in the Marcellus Shale, residents have widely differing opinions on whether hydrofracking is a good idea. Many environmental groups believe it should not be permitted anywhere in the state. On the other hand, some farmers who are struggling to make a living would benefit from the money they would make by leasing their land to drilling companies. New York Governor Andrew Cuomo (above) has the tough job of deciding what to do. He hopes to restrict hydrofracking to areas where local communities support it.

What Happened Where?

Grand Coulee Dam ▪

The Grand Coulee Dam, constructed across the Columbia River in eastern Washington, is the largest electric power–producing facility in the world.

California is one of the country's leaders in the development of solar power, wind power, and other forms of renewable energy.

CA

he Barnett Shale, in Texas, was the st shale gas deposit where hydrofracking chnology was used successfully. The ale rocks in this deposit are more than 0 million years old.

→ **Barnett Shale**

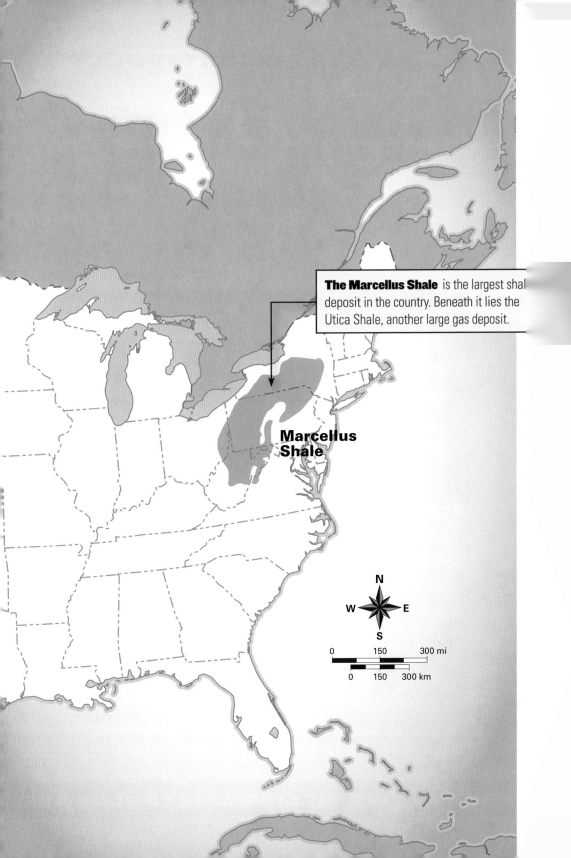

The Marcellus Shale is the largest shal deposit in the country. Beneath it lies the Utica Shale, another large gas deposit.

Marcellus
Shale

N
W E
S

0   150   300 mi

0   150   300 km

Using Energy Wisely

Hydrofracking will likely continue to be a controversial issue in the years to come.

It's no secret that hydrofracking has created a lot of controversy. Some people believe that it has the potential to do serious harm to the environment. Others think that this technology offers the best way to provide people with reliable and affordable energy for years to come.

Despite these different views, it is a fact that Americans need energy. And as the country's population grows, we will need even more of it. All fossil fuels will eventually run out. Renewable sources such as the sun, wind, geothermal heat, water, and biomass are likely to be the energy sources of the future. In the meantime, we should do all we can to use energy wisely. Here are just a few ways to do that:

Replace regular lightbulbs with compact fluorescent bulbs and light-emitting diodes. Both use less energy and last longer than regular bulbs. Heat up food in the microwave instead of the regular oven whenever possible. Turn off the TV, computer, and lights when you're not using them. Unplug computer and cell phone chargers from the wall when they are not being used. Save hot water by taking short showers instead of baths. Ride your bike or walk instead of taking the car.

Remember, we can help protect our planet's future by using less energy, no matter where that energy comes from.

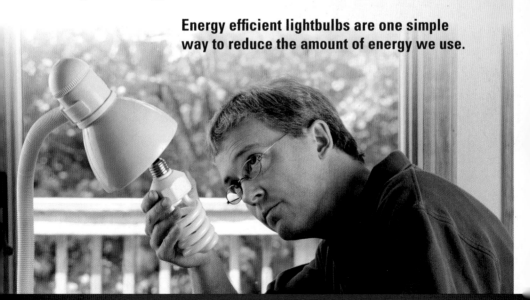

Energy efficient lightbulbs are one simple way to reduce the amount of energy we use.

SOLD EACH YEAR IN THE UNITED STATES.

Andrew Cuomo

George Mitchell (1919–) is the man responsible for the boom in natural gas drilling in the world today. He was trained as a geologist and started his own gas drilling company after World War II. In the 1980s, he began to explore hydrofracking as a way to get more gas out of his drilling sites. After years of experimenting, he finally figured out how to extract shale gas through hydrofracking. By the time he retired and sold his company, he was a billionaire several times over.

Dick Cheney (1941–) served as the 46th vice president of the United States, from 2001 to 2009, under President George W. Bush. Before taking office, Cheney held a variety of positions, including secretary of defense and chief executive officer of Halliburton, a large energy and oil field services company. While in office, he supported many programs that promoted oil and gas exploration in the United States.

Andrew Cuomo (1957–) was elected governor of New York in 2010. Because New York is the site of major potential hydrofracking sites, Cuomo's position on the topic will play a major role in the state's future. He has said that he hopes to restrict fracking only to communities where it is approved by residents.

Barack Obama (1961–) is the 44th president of the United States. He believes the country should reduce its dependence on imported energy. During his presidency, U.S. foreign oil imports have dropped, while total oil production has increased. He supports expanding natural gas drilling in the United States but also expresses concern about the effects of hydrofracking on the environment.

Barack Obama

Josh Fox (1972–) is a film director whose 2010 documentary *Gasland* brought new attention to the controversy surrounding hydrofracking. Since the film's release, Fox has become one of the nation's most visible opponents of hydrofracking.

Josh Fox

TIMELINE

1660s

Early American settlers notice "burning springs" throughout Appalachia.

1820

Salt well drillers accidentally find natural gas in Pennsylvania and Ohio.

1952

New York City receives natural gas for the first time.

1980s

Mitchell Energy begins to experiment with hydrofracking as a way of obtaining natural gas trapped in shale deposits.

1821

The first deep natural gas well is drilled in Erie, Pennsylvania.

1947

The first natural gas hydraulic fracturing experiment is done in Kansas.

2011

The Environmental Protection Agency finds that chemicals used in hydrofracking are the likely cause of contaminated water supplies in Pavillion, Wyoming.

France becomes the first country to ban hydrofracking.

LIVING HISTORY

Primary sources provide firsthand evidence about a topic. Witnesses to a historical event create primary sources. They include autobiographies, newspaper reports of the time, oral histories, photographs, and memoirs. A secondary source analyzes primary sources, and is one step or more removed from the event. Secondary sources include textbooks, encyclopedias, and commentaries. To view the following primary and secondary sources, go to www.factsfornow.scholastic.com. Enter the keyword **Hydrofracking** and look for the Living History logo Σ.

Σ **FrackNation** Documentary films are a good way of letting people know about controversial issues such as hydrofracking. After hearing from people directly involved with an issue, viewers can decide for themselves what to believe.

Σ President Obama's 2012 State of the Union Address

Every year, the president of the United States addresses Congress to report on the condition of the nation and outline his plans for the coming year. Among the topics President Obama discussed in his 2012 address was his support for development of the country's oil and gas resources.

Σ A Report on Chemicals Used in Hydraulic Fracturing

Governmental committees, such as the U.S. House of Representatives Committee on Energy and Commerce, gather information on many issues that affect the American people. In 2011, this committee launched an investigation of the chemicals used in hydrofracking.

Σ A UN Report on Renewable Energy Sources The United

Nations Environmental Programme's Intergovernmental Panel on Climate Change put together a report focusing on renewable energy sources and the prevention of climate change.

RESOURCES

Books

Iwinski, Melissa. *The Wind at Work*. New York: Children's Press, 2007.

Rigsby, Mike. *Doable Renewables: 16 Alternative Energy Projects for Young Scientists*. Chicago: Chicago Review Press, 2010.

Walker, Niki. *Generating Wind Power*. New York: Crabtree Publishing, 2007.

Visit this Scholastic Web site for more information on hydrofracking: www.factsfornow.scholastic.com Enter the keyword Hydrofracking

GLOSSARY

aquifers (AH-kwih-furz) underground layers of rock, sand, or gravel where water is stored

evaporates (i-VAP-uh-rayts) changes into a vapor or gas

flammable (FLAM-uh-buhl) quick to catch fire and burn

fossil fuels (FAH-suhl FYOOLZ) coal, oil, or natural gas, formed from the remains of prehistoric animals and plants

generators (JEN-uh-ray-turz) machines that produce electricity by turning a magnet inside a coil of wire

global warming (GLOH-buhl WAR-ming) a gradual rise in the temperature of the earth's atmosphere, caused by human activities that pollute

greenhouse gas (GREEN-hous GAS) a gas such as carbon dioxide or methane that contributes to the warming of Earth

organic (or-GAN-ik) from or produced by living things

permeable (PUR-mee-uh-buhl) having pores or openings that permit liquids or gases to pass through

sedimentary rock (sed-uh-MEN-tuh-ree RAHK) rock that is formed from many layers of sand, mud, or other sediment that is pressed together over many years

seismographs (SIZE-muh-grafs) instruments that detect earthquakes and measure their power

INDEX

Page numbers in *italics* indicate illustrations.

ABOUT THE AUTHOR

Ann O. Squire was trained as an animal behaviorist. She has written many books about animals and other natural science topics. Before becoming an author, she studied the behavior of laboratory rats, tropical fish in the Caribbean, and electric fish from central Africa. Her favorite part of being a writer is the chance to learn as much as she can about all sorts of topics. She lives in Katonah, New York.